The Saint of Everything

The Saint of Everything

poems | DEBORAH KEENAN

Lynx House Press

Spokane, Washington

Acknowledgments

The author wishes to thank the editors of the following publications in which the poems in this volume originally appeared:

American Literary Review: "Two Stones," "The Thief," and "Garage"

casinolitmag.com: "The Saint of Common Murders Makes the List"

Cimarron Review: "The Saint of Abandoned Nurseries"

Clackamas Literary Review, 20th Anniversary Issue: "Tenderness"

Midway Journal: "Burchfield in the Moonlight," "Tiny Homage to Cornell," "Young Wolves"

Smartish Pace: "The Saint of Everything"

Sugar House Review: "After the Shipwreck"

The Under Review: "For Some Reason in our Elementary School"

Tin House: "The Heartland, Where the Secrets Are" and "Animals Above Me"

Water-Stone Review: "The Saint of Childhood Says No to the Dreamland Tree," "There's Nothing Wrong"

"One of the Old Songs" *Body of Evidence,* Laurel Poetry Collective (Anthology), Poetry City, U.S.A. Volume Three, Low Brow Press

"Animals Above Me" selected for poets.org, Academy of American Poets

"Horizon," "The Dream World of Memory," "She Loved the Mountains," "After Just Storms," "Write the Word Liar Twelve Times," "No Longer a Crime Scene," "The Green Lights Say Yes in the City at Night," "They Ran in the Autumn Rain," "Not Betrayal," and "Not Too Far From Home," published in a limited edition chapbook, *So She Had the World,* a book in collaboration with the painter Susan Solomon, Red Bird Chapbooks

"The Lion in the Dunes," *Body of Evidence,* Laurel Poetry Collective, (Anthology)

"The Story that Covers the Story," *Body of Evidence,* Laurel Poetry Collective, (Anthology)

"Keep Making a Map of the World," *Bringing Gifts, Bringing News,* Downstairs Press

FIRST EDITION

Cover Art: Charles Gurche
Author Photo: Emily Cook
Book and Jacket Design: Christine Lysnewycz Holbert

ISBN 978-0-89924-189-0

LYNX HOUSE PRESS books are distributed by Washington State University Press, wsupress@wsu.edu

LIBRARY OF CONGRESS CATALOGING-IN-PUBLICATION DATA is available from the Library of Congress

Table of Contents

for Aisling, Ezi, Manni, and Rosalind

The Thief

He came into our home and found the ball of string
I used to tie up tall flowers and climbing beans and peas
in the summer. He created
an intricate web that crossed through the kitchen
into the dining room, and ended the web tied
to a nail hammered into the mantel where we hung our son's
Christmas stocking. He chose from my bureau
slips, bras, panties, and the cream-colored nylons
that had been resting in their old-fashioned box,
waiting for the right occasion. He hung all these things
from the string and the forms made odd shadows in our home.
In the basement he went through all my photos
in the darkroom and chose his favorites (I think)
and clipped them to the string with my clothespins.
One was a picture of our son, in a gleaming white t-shirt;
in the photo he was just two years old, the same smile that breaks
and warms a heart now. He went through my poems and crossed out
the ones he hated with black magic marker.
He took our son's second favorite blanket,
two pillows from the couch, all the cans of soup,
the white and brown rice, the hammer
and the saw. He left a note saying *I am telling you*
how to live. Now live that way.

Horizon

My neighbor needed a lot of trees to block the horizon line.
The prairie too suggestive, reeking of ideas and places
he might travel. He planted poplars first, because they loved
the wind, then cottonwoods for snow in June, then firs
in a kind of motionless curve around his property.
He still loved the world in a few ways, so to the south
he left the road up to his place alone, let the wildflowers
fill the ditches, gave himself a view of whoever might drive
or walk towards him. After he'd had the life
he'd been told was his, the one he deserved,
he hired a small crew to remove the poplars,
the cottonwoods, the firs. After their many days
of work, and the parade of trucks carrying
the trees away, the wind could finally get at
the house, the man, the shining windows.
The horizon was blunt and easy on his eyes,
a line drawn in gold, then green, then charcoal.
A child might have drawn that line, another
life might have happened here.

The Lion in the Dunes

Of course he is lost.
Not a tree, not a pride,
not a river, not even
an oasis for comfort.
He is brave, or angry
or longing for solitude.
He is old, or alone,
or weary of the rules
he lives by.
He is filthy with sand,
grit in his eyes.
The desert wind lifts
and shakes his golden
mane. He is not
aware of being a
symbol of anything,
no hermetic truths
swirl around him.
And though he is
part of the book
of the world
he does not know that.
He follows the carved
and glowing wall
of the dune
and his paw prints
make no path to follow
as he leans into
the wind, always
his one true love.

Making the Map of the World

"It was a windy, whispering, moonless night.
To guide himself, he opened under a lamp
a map he had brought. The breeze ruffled
and fluttered it, but he could see enough
to decide on the direction he should take
to reach the heart of the place."

—Thomas Hardy, *Jude the Obscure*

To understand another's map of the world—our duty, fear, and joy.
To walk out into the windy, whispering, moonless night,
To carry the lamp without complaint.

Animals Above Me

My neighbor cradles a coyote at the top of the hill behind my house.
She is screaming at me to stop being so afraid.
Then the keening yet ecstatic cry of our neighborhood hawk, and then
The plunge, the lift, the rabbit, crying.
Worst, the nightly dreams of the snake, huge, yellow and green,
On the high shelving in my old house, sometimes the bedroom,
Sometimes the dining room. The dream makes me sick
And I wake from it every night between 3:30 and 4:00. Comforting
Books do not comfort, so I get up exhausted and start the day.
Other neighbors keep telling me: as long as you see it, you don't need
To be afraid. Then in the next dream, I cannot see it.
I am sick and afraid. I wake up again.
The bear straddling my maple tree, about twenty feet up.
Is he scared?
I am so sick of thinking about how safe I am, so sick of making
Animals carry all my fear. The human beings in our country,
Half at least, live in terror. In our world, half, at least,
Terrified, desperate, sick with fear. I see it. I cannot see it.
I see it.

The Dream World of Memory

The woman fell from the ladder and her beauty
sustained her even as blood from her forehead
and shoulder seeped into the white carpet.
The visitor in the home knew nothing
of the beautiful woman,
her city, but wrapped her head
and shoulder in towels, carried her
to the car, sat with her in the emergency
room, comforted her, stayed by her side.

The dog lay by the side of the road
but she was brave enough, years later,
to lift the dog into the front seat of her car,
and find a vet, even as she heard the dog's
breathing slow. She drove with one hand
on the wheel , one hand deep in
golden fur. Yes, this dog lived.

Comforted by these memories,
she built them as a fortress
around later acts
of cowardice.
It was no use, though,
drama and injury
and injustice surrounded
her, forced her back
into the lives of the suffering
strangers, pushed her
to reach her hands

toward the broken
animals she found there.
Inside the dream world
of memory she lived—
coward, sometimes forgiven,
brave, but never, she thought,
through her own choice.
A mysterious life, just like
everyone else's.

Hospital

At the hospital my head and shoulders exist
inside a plastic tent. A box of ice, replenished every few
hours, at the back of my head, outside the tent. The plastic
is unzipped three times a day for meals. Four times a day
I get shots in the ass, the hip, the outer thigh. Don't cry.
Blood taken from small veins hidden in closed elbows.
When told to extend my arms, I obey. I'm awfully good,
though it does not make the nurses love me.

There's one window in the door to my room. My mother
can come as far as the outside of the door, position her face
in the window. Then the nurse shakes my leg to rouse
me. I turn to the window and see my mother's face
through the wall of plastic tent, and one glass window.
This is the face I love and wait for, and one of the reasons
the nurses do not fuss over me. So, this is protected memory.
No evidence saved, just one truth from the olden days,
and the three times I lived for days and nights in this kind
of quarantine. What grew from this garden? Claustrophobia,
fear, loneliness, bravery, stoicism, the animal ability to abide?

She Loved the Mountains

She had a lot of vertical energy.
She likes the tops of things:
crests of waves, tea pot lids,
the softest hair on a baby's head.

She was never afraid on mountain
roads, took the curves, wanted
to find the old lodges,
wanted to see how weather
reclaimed the front porches,
the old, stripped-bare timber,
always hoped some mountain
lion would be waiting
in one of the guest rooms.

She thought her spirit
always ascended, she believed
in almost all religions that
made good use of the sky.
She was kind of holy,
a kind of sacred person,
really, though rarely
noticed. She lived
a long time,
and then didn't
participate much
in her dying.
Indifferent, radiant,
then gone.

Garage

White bike leans against the north wall of the blue garage,
unharmed after my father drives the car into its east wall,
the wall unmoored, angled, the saws and hammers
jumping from their assigned places, the heavy clatter as
the engine revs and smokes and the mother, in her swirl
of bedclothes, cries out, wrenches the car door open.

Years go by and I see the circle of the steering wheel
holding him in place as the fresh air in the middle of the night
enters the garage. Oh, he's deeply drunk and deeply asleep
and it is terrible to wake him, terrible to let him sleep.

It's pointless to resist memory.
White bike, gleaming saw, a neighbor's voice, an owl's call.
A simple arrival into an east wall on a moonlit night
and how it took his whole life to sleep this way.

Tiny Homage to Cornell

Here, for Cornell, I make
my smallest collage.
From a nature magazine
published in the '50s
I cut this patch
of wild grass,
still humming with
greens and browns,
because four color
printing was just that ideal then,
still humming, following the rules
of still lifes,
with the lion who walked out
of the photo just in time,
and I've taken one doll
from the pages of
my mother's scrapbook
trimmed the mold,
restored her,
perched her in my cut out
U-shape of the grass.
She is not imprisoned
in any way.
She's free to leave,
which eases the tension
of the homage completely.

She just balances,
the cream of her gown
matching the sticks
in the grass.

Saint of Sleep

All he does, nothing else.
Halo the smallest nightlight,
halo jaunty for the big time sleepers,
hidden in curls for those afraid
to close their eyes. Some jobs
the saint of sleep turns down:
saint of mothers, saint of the harvest,
saint of piano players, saint
of those stranded in windstorms.
He rejects all natural and cultural drama.
Saint of sleep touches my love
on his forehead. Saint of sleep
takes him deep, past white noise,
past airplane drone and pilot voice,
takes him to the cave of sleep,
the mountain of sleep, the prairie
of sleep. Saint of sleep wants
to protect all heartbroken, sobbing
babies, all sleep deprived, ramped up
parents, and all those who work
too hard for too long. Like most
saints, his halo rests heavy
on his head. He had no idea
how far from home and his own bed
his saintly choice would carry him.

The Saint of Childhood Says No to the Dreamland Tree

No to the shaking no to the guarding of sheep.
No to the lullaby and goodnight No to sweet and low,
sweet and low.
No to the old mill steam, no.
No to the curtains opened or closed, no
to the nightlight shaped like a crescent moon.
No to talk of tomorrow. No to four saints
at the four corners of the bed. No
to the land of counterpane, no
to the murmur of older voices
in the next room. No to the real
linden tree outside the southern
window, no always no,
to the Dreamland tree.

Young Wolves

Running up from the railroad tracks, crossing the bridge,
no cars on the avenue except mine. Five in the morning,
two wolves, one car, one woman.
I drive slowly in the dark, hit my brakes,
gray fur fluttering as they run in front of my car,
as the wind blows from the south, gives them something
mild and invisible to run into. Child wolves,
get out of the city before sunrise, consider the times
we live in. Keep running.

For Some Reason, in Our Elementary School

Dodgeball was called War.
We played the game so happily,
With such violence, black eyes,
Sprained fingers and wrists,
A ball snapped my head back
And my body followed. Knocked
Out against the gym wall
I was so still my best friend
Ran crying to the nurse's office
As the game continued.
What a gift, this wild, vicious game,
All of us little kids in my suburb,
And only some of us knew violence
At home, the doors closed,
But here on the court
In a game we called War
We reveled in our primal
Instincts to hit, to hurt, to survive,
To be finally alone, triumphant
On the wooden floor.
The nurse slapped me back
To consciousness and whatever
Dream I'd been having
Was lost forever.

Burchfield and His Wallpaper

I found the wallpaper design in my research and understood how I had been claimed many years before. For a brief time, Burchfield lived in New York City and designed wallpaper. Not a happy time for him, though productive. I came home from summer camp when I was eight, and my mother had wallpapered my small bedroom. The pattern was birches and leaves. I loved it. When my Aunt Loretta moved in with my mom, after my Uncle Ben died, we re-did my old bedroom for her. Burchfield's pattern gone. I miss that wallpaper. I miss those two women, that small house on the dead end street. Burchfield reminds me to go back, to not lose my memories, to respect their power. All the houses I've painted and drawn for so many years look nothing like Burchfield's mystical houses. He's one ghost I try and stay responsive to, though I am very busy remembering things and trying not to remember things.

After Just Enough Storms

The creek's wild, eating the banks,
the cone flowers pulled loose,
their dusty pink petals tiny arrows
in the rush of it all. Trees that risked
life on the edge fall, instant bridges
for the foolish, and the watercress
beds gleam green under the rollicking
current. Oh, it's a kind of heaven
you can't be dismissed from
by any angel in love with dust
or prairie. You might even pray
that the storms keep coming.
That the quiet creek of late
autumn will always and only be
a private memory. You might
hope to sit on this bench,
be finally swept away
and carried to safety.

Goldenrod in November

Fluttering ghost shapes in every field gone wild:
it seems Burchfield had such faith in his palette,
faith in gray and white. Whenever he saw spirit,
he stopped and painted it.
I bow down to his sureness,
how knowledge seemed to burden and enlighten him.
How like the sun the goldenrod is in
its glory, never mind
its terrible reputation, never mind
the men and women with torches aflame,
and silver scythes
Approaching from all edges of the field
To destroy it.

Not Yet

Those days, when we let the white tiger rest
On the lawn, dared the neighbors to complain—
Those days are gone—we never imagined
Living through eras, so happily reckless, yet
So peaceful about dying young and happy.
In our confusion we never imagined
The tiger would choose another family,
Never thought of our world without him.

Now, we feel a bit like the bobbing pelicans, the cormorants
Perched on the wires, though we, so earth-bound,
Slump against window sills,
And watch as the small sleek Florida panthers,
Somehow back from almost extinction, roam
Our lawn, sleep in our trees, wake, look down
At our small children. Their eyes golden
With a kind of hunger, they paw so gently
And insistently at our front door, but we
Haven't let them in, not yet.

Write the Word Liar Twelve Times

On a white metal post in front of the abandoned gas station.
Write with your finger into the dust and grime on the front window:
I need gas before I get on the freeway to visit my grandma.
Why are you closed?

Into the gravel and dirt outside the locked bathroom door write in huge
block letters: *HELP ME. SEE ME FROM THE AIR.*

You won't get far. Not to the freeway, that's for sure.
You can name twelve liars by heart. Or you can name
the twelve lies the liar told you.
You might not see your grandma again, and a kind
of desperate sadness sweeps through the prairie grasses
toward you.

You lied to her once, only, but you're just the fool
who never plans ahead, never fills the gas tank, who
can't make it to the freeway ramp.

Who were you going to be? This is the question
that haunts your days and nights. You're out of gas
now, so lock your car and start walking.
In the olden days, someone safe would stop, give you
a lift with no price to pay.

The Saint of Common Murders Makes the List

She couldn't tell the truth. She was the queen of liars and at least ten people
wanted her to die.

He was cruel because it gave him pleasure. One hundred people wanted him
   to die.

She was very old and quite a few people wanted her to die.

She was just a baby, but so plain, born to beautiful narcissists who both wanted
her to die.

He was never amusing and often drunk and several people wanted him to die.

She was a terrible mother, with twelve children, and only one of the twelve
didn't want her to die.

He was kind. Eight million people and animals wanted him to live,
but two million people and animals wanted him to die.

She cultivated a false innocence long past the time to give up on innocence
and one person finally admitted he wanted her to die.

All were murdered, and only one is not a cold case.

The Heartland, Where the Secrets Are

The couple found the body caught in a fallen tree.
She was not a toddler; she had the grown-up beauty
of a four-year-old. The couple who found her wept.
They had coveted her, hated the couple
who made her, dear little afterthought, dear
little worshipped one, 12th of the 12, and only
the second girl. They did not call the cops.
One waded into the creek, pulled the little girl
away from the arms of the tree, pulled the girl
close and handed her to the other. That one
lifted her and laid her in a hollow the deer
had made. The girl's little blue sweater was held
in place by a knife piercing the sweater and the girl
at heart level. The couple said a brief prayer
and covered her with leaves. In the heartland
there are many murderers, and most go unnamed
and free. The couple waited for the snow
to cover her small body.

No Longer a Crime Scene

Little chance to become a shrine.
The yellow tape torn down
snakes and shivers in the tall grass.
The rain everyone prayed for came,
and the blood raced down the hillside.
Those who mourn are right now
at the fantastic funeral, the gleaming
casket, the tearful goodbyes,
the promises to never forget.

No longer a crime scene,
the land is calm, as it always was,
the murderer on his way
to another place, loyal
to his one murder, sure
he won't be tempted again.

Tenderness

Skating at night alone
the field flooded
no wind no snow
disturbed the calm
freezing and the one
who was once a friend
skated past then circled
then placed his arms
in that old diagonal way
took her hands

The body memories
inside the two who
could not be friends
woke and they came
together circled
the field now perfectly
frozen their blades cut
with only a faint shaping
sound
they did not harm
the ice

they skated and surrendered
to the end of their friendship
serene and shocked
by the winter portrait
they had hoped
never to create.

Two Stones

Pick up one stone. You can carry it. You can carry it a long way.
Pick up the second stone. You can carry it.
These are the only two stones some people want you to carry.
There are the two stones some people pick up as children
and never put down.
If you only have to carry one stone, sometimes you can put it down,
move to the seashore, forget the stone.
If you only have to carry one or the other, you might be all right.
But some people want you to carry both.
And because of how you were raised, you are eager to please.
You seem to be a volunteer-yes, please let me carry both stones.
That is how they see you, that you are someone who wants to carry both.
It doesn't matter that these two stones are killing you. That you know it.
You are pretty much always carrying one or the other.
They are heavier each passing year.
Imagining being old and alone with your two stones makes you weep,
though your crying doesn't win any hearts for you.
So, there you go, with your two stones. You are not an allegory
or a sketch or even a narrative. And those who love metaphor
don't want to hear this one.
You carry two stones, and you never put them down.

The Story That Covers the Story

A friend sits vigil with her dying mother.
They have not hidden their lives from each other
so there is not much to say. Sometimes light
comes in the window, sometimes they rest
in darkness. Both wonder if now is the time
to tell the secret stories. They hope, as all storytellers
do, that the long-protected stories will keep each other
alive, but the secret stories, lively and entombed,
keep breathing inside my friend, her mother,
and they matter too much to tell. Each woman
feels the peace that comes from protecting
the secret stories; they both know that death
is coming, and there's not much to say.

Burchfield in the Moonlight

The painters who paint by moonlight
belong to a secret group of the living
and the dead. Burchfield sees Ryder
at a canvas in the almost dark.
He weeps to see his hero
in the shadows, at work
on a depiction of a purified night tree,
It is terribly lonely under the light
of the moon. When the living
painters see one of their dead
at work, it inspires but hurts
them, too. When one of the dead
sees another dead artist
at work,
there are almost always tears.

The Houses, Streets, the Slanted Rain, the Snowstorms, the Machinery of America

the fields and the valleys, the trees alone and trees gathered together, the light in the sky, and the light in windows curtained and uncurtained, the church steeples and graveyards, the faces in the center of flowers, the owls that fly and those that are still, the Milky Way, the dreams we struggle to wake from, and the dreams we court, the animals Burchfield paints with care, not love, the animals I cannot paint, the mysterious bird and all the roads out of town, Orion and the abandoned farmhouses, telephone poles and trees and trees and trees. He and I grow up, suffer, love, and admit everything is breathing.

Oh, the Blues

These blues, this wheat field,
a family owns this Burchfield,
friends of his. I am the kind
of person who wouldn't have known
how to be Burchfield's friend.
I know his spirit would have been
too much for me.
So I am feeling it today, the weight of art,
the pressure, certain days I can't let it
give me any relief, I can't stay in the moment
of the work of art because it wipes me out,
it hurts me and I believe I can't handle
this version of pain. Oh, the blues,
in Wheatfield and Tower, the blues
are all I want, and the long view to the horizon,
I want that, too. And I want this pressure
to leave my body and spirit alone.
So many blues in this painting.
I'm a little dizzy thinking
about his work.
I'm seeing how
he got to me, I'm admitting it all
today.

Sun, Moon, and Star

In this painting by Burchfield there's a kind of gesture
towards happiness. As our eyes find the sun, the moon,
and the star we're back inside beloved children's books,
the memories of how we learned to see.
I walk down his street, at peace with his usual rusts
and creams, grays and dull golds. I want to think
he was just fine the days and nights he painted this,
that the sun, moon, and star gave their light to him
and he understood this light was privilege and joy.

Me and Monica Vitti

I took all the January film courses I could in college
so I could study foreign movies with professors
who just wanted to sit in the dark and teach students
to love what they loved.
Truly, it seemed a miracle to me that I could sit
in my winter coat in the cold viewing room
and watch movies with subtitles.
This weekend my daughter and son-in-law
brought over a picture of Monica Vitti
and asked who she reminded me of.
The answer, which I didn't guess, was me.
Same hairdo, same nose, a similar kind
of beauty we had in our twenties, gone
but not forgotten, and this is the daughter
who would remember that beauty, child
of my twenties. I taped the picture into
my new artist notebook, stared
at Monica Vitti, traveled back to
the screening room of my college days,
remembering how I felt, day after day,
sitting out January in Minnesota,
so full of gratitude, and longing to leave America.

The Green Lights Say Yes in the City at Night

He was still a walker in the city, new to the country.
A neighbor caught his arm as he was about to step into the street:
Red means no, don't go. Do you understand?
The neighbor thought himself full of virtue, a life saved,
Special virtue, since the life saved belonged to a stranger
He did not love.

The stranger in the country studied the streetlights,
The threads and clots of other humans gathered at the corners,
Learned the mystery of the yellow light, saw only the reckless,
The young, race for the other side. Saw red stop all
But the foolish, and he was not a fool anymore.

Late at night the green lights said yes, and he measured
His new life by those green lights. When rain fell,
The green lights turned the raindrops to green lines
And those lines steadied him and he gave up his bewilderment
And his loneliness, most of it, as the years went by.

Keep Making the Map of the World

The shells look like antiquated musical instruments
no one plays anymore.
Not decorative. Not useful
spirit guides.

Place the best shells in the center
of every continent you believe in.

Use the map to make the shells
fill with meaning.

What about this map matters enough
to keep it visible?

The old shells thought
their work was done,
shocked to be touched again.

Reasons

We want them to know the real
reasons for what they feel,
the weight of it all.
We think if they know
the reasons, then the world
will feel less theirs, less something
to guard, less something
to be too careful with.
We keep busy talking.
We say, the moon is just the moon
the mechanics of the earth
won't break down on their watch.
We take pictures of everything
in the world that doesn't need them
We want them to be on their way,
less sick with worry, but gone.

The Shield

He drew a picture of the shield to carry into battle.
He drew a helmet with a plumed feather.
He drew space-age guns that he colored gold and silver.
He grew up slowly, then quickly.
 On the field of battle he was a friend and the one
they called the artist.
On the field of battle he tried to shield others,
and others shielded him.
He drew pictures of men and women he served with
and they scanned them, sent them as documents
to their lovers and families. He was very tired.
He played solitaire on quiet nights, and drew pictures
of his future, and carried those pictures, folded,
into every battle.
He became exactly the person he planned to be
all those years before, sitting in the sunlight
at the dining room table, drawing his shield.

The Saint of Maps Tries to Help

> "We have no map;
> Possibly we will never reach haven,
> heaven."
>
> —H.D., "The Walls Do Not Fall," section 43

The saint of maps is not romantic.
He wants to help, but he is not the saint
of patience, not the saint of wanderers
who refuse his help.
He knows the way to heaven,
unfolds his map for them,
to show them the clear markings
others have followed
but he did not appear to them
in a blaze of fire and glory—
he's no angel, and the wanderers
turn away.
Heaven must be harder to find,
they're sure of that, and leave him
folding his map. Perhaps if they had seen
his tears falling in anger and frustration
he might have reminded them of the fathers
they once loved, he might have convinced them
he knew the way.

After the Shipwreck

Paradise can't have people, so they all died.
The wooden sides of the ship bleached in the sun,
smoothed by waves, were salvaged
by artists on their way to another island.
The paintings done on this soft wood
have lasted over four hundred years now.
Curators feel their hands tingle, shake, when allowed
to hang the paintings in their museums.
The wandering artists died so long ago,
Just like the sailors before them.
Not shipwrecked, no drama, they lived
Together and one by one died.
They knew their best work had been painted
on the wood from the ship, and though
careless in so many ways, they protected
the paintings, which hang in all the great
museums, anonymous and brilliant.

Three Things I Asked My Friend

We crossed the Howling Wind Bridge on our weekly walk.
I asked, "When I am in a rock and roll band called Shelter Dogs
will you come to all my shows?"
I asked, "When I am in a rock and roll band called The Dancing
Caucasians, will you buy my CDs?"
I asked, "If I painted our figures very small, crossing the bridge
in ferocious wind, with blazing trees taking up most of the canvas,
would you buy that painting for one million dollars?"
The great thing about this friendship is he said yes, and yes, and yes.

They Ran in the Autumn Rain

Two coyotes.
Four black horses, two with human riders.
Seven people on the avenue, their dogs beside them.
The mother, hearing the cry of her son, ran outside to save him,
though he had been gone for years.
The kids on the block, after seeing one of their own with a blue umbrella,
and then the street was full of children.
The fox and her babies, from the garden where they had been feasting.
The wedding party, from the crest of the hill, the bride's veil floating,
then transformed by raindrops.
The broken-hearted one. Trying to forgive herself.
I saw her stop running. Lift her face to the warm rain.

A Better Promise

> "The landscapist does not lose himself into the forest without
> a gleam of light under its furthest branches, nor venture out in rain
> unless he may somewhere pierce to a better promise in the distance,
> or cling to some closing gap of variable blue above."
>
> —John Ruskin, *Modern Painters*

Our son loves the forest where dappled light moves, and trees are distinct
and underbrush seems to have been cleared by the hand of God.
We stop in this place, where the creek is murmur or roar, depending
on the day, the season. We just stop, love this particular place on our walk.
We say, *if a mountain lion came down the hill we could see it clearly.*
We say, *if deer were on the move we'd see each flutter of tail, each flinch
of ear as they realized we stood close by.* Sometimes I believe we are
held graciously in the moment, that the distance means
nothing to us. Sometimes I believe we are each thinking
of the better promise.

The Butterflies

They were there all the time, and this shocked me.
The beauty available at the window, hours at a time, felt new
to me, different than what I have in my hidden city garden,
different than my two pines, the plain daisies, planted first
in honor of Jeannette, whom I loved, whom I imagined would live
forever—that way we feel about the good people we meet
when we are young.

The butterflies lived on in my memory. I wrote poems about them,
I let them become part of my spiritual life, prayed they would always
be there, outside their dining room window in Virginia, that state
with my mother's name, thought of them in their powerful lives.

Who Are the Animals With You in Times of Jubilation?

Cats, kittens, lions and tigers,
brown horses, palominos,
and the oldest circus horse in America.
One dog, who represents all the dogs
loved by people I love,
who represents the one dog I loved.
Are birds animals? I never remember.
If they are, then cardinals, gold finches,
blackbirds, crows, rooks, and ravens.
If they are, then egrets, cranes,
and beloved pelicans with their treasure
box bodies.
These are the animals I want with me
in my time of jubilation. This is my answer
to the question I asked one winter night
in one of my classes, which I don't remember
any of my students answering.

The Saint of Abandoned Nurseries

Not babies. Plants, trees, and flowers.
Susan and I would go there when the mood
and the day matched. Hidden away,
off a freeway built for a suburb that never happened,
as if the thought of all that land outside the city
made the contractors weary, the idea of all
those people appalling.
The man who owned it had a past,
and a small staff of ex-cons, or not,
maybe just renegades, secret citizens
in the country of bits of nature for sale.
The whole nursery was wrapped in heavy plastic,
old cats wandered the wet floors, stepping
with delicate feet over the green hoses,
ignoring the mice skittering between the flowers.
It was so easy to be there. All the plants
dripping, and the few customers sweating
under the plastic. The owner counted
the plants, and if we bought enough he'd point
to some tables near the cash register, say
You can choose free flowers from those tables
because you two are great customers. And we were.
Giant geodes rested on the shelf behind him,
and huge pieces of red and gold glass.
He was a good guy, exhausted by freedom.
They shut him down, something about back taxes,
or other plants growing under plastic where customers
weren't allowed. The saint of abandoned nurseries
guards the place now. She walks the aisles.

She rounded up the old cats months ago,
took them to the humane society, though
she knew how few people would choose them,
but she's the saint of abandoned nurseries,
not cats, so she doesn't dream of the cats too often.
She takes her knife and slices through the plastic,
lets the wind and rain come in.

Returning at the End of Suffering

The deer, the spotted leopard,
The sleek sharks, the maroon starfish.
Yes, we were surprised.
Then the Siberian tigers
Came through the broken
Forest, and then two girls.
Maybe eight or nine.
We walked toward them,
Making human assumptions,
But they belonged
To the tigers now,
And so we let them go.
Choose your kingdom,
Choose your species.
New rules at the end of suffering.

Not Betrayal

Nothing in the world is betraying us.
Not the late spring, not the gray days,
not the wonderful liars in office,
not the friends who broke our hearts.
Nothing in our easy lives
works against us, not the river,
carrying its burden of uprooted trees,
and the ghosts of those who had to let go
of the bridge railings, not the families,
who can't see us clearly, not the mirrors
we try to avoid, those shiny truth tellers.
It's pretty bad, those days when we see
there's no betrayal anywhere, and
it's simply more days, more nights,
and what we plan to do with them.

Not Too Far From Home

The prairie waits, little bluestem, country rivers, pastures
    and gleaming black cows.
Invisible coyotes, and the guide wheels the wooden buffalo
    into the shed for the night.
Petroglyphs emerge from ancient rock face, and she considers
    the patience
of the artists. They are calm, driving the country roads,
    she considers another life
that might have been hers. Two hawks, one for each of them.
    She belongs to the city
now, but here, not too far from home, they hear the adamant machinery
    of the gravel
quarry, witness the crazy resurrection of wildflowers they haven't seen
    since they were
children, take the long prairie path back to the car as the heat
    presses their shoulders,
and the wind touches the day, touches the prairie grass.

Blue Fish Nights

Lucky, all those blue fish nights,
sunsets we missed because of the blue fish,
white rice, corn on the cob, crazy salads,
weren't we lucky, the nights we raced
to Corn Hill to see the sunsets, the table
barely cleared, who's coming, who's staying
behind to read a book, play an album
on the stereo, take one more quick shower
hoping to ease what the sun did,
what riding the waves at Long Nook did,
yet so hard to leave that shoreline, then
easy, knowing blue fish was waiting, and someone
got more corn and someone got more milk
because when we were all there
we were a crowd, a gathering, a group,
a family, and runs to the grocery
were epic, oh, we were lucky
to have the blue fish nights,
Larry grilling, and the years passed,
then another baby in the old high chair,
then that baby grew, and then one,
and then two more, and then another,
high chair dragged out of the shed,
along with broken beach umbrellas,
plastic beach toys, and on it went
and on it goes,
time slowed, time racing,
not perfect, but human,
and lucky,
and remembered.

These Days

> "The fire we made such a fuss about turned out to be a rainbow.
> Already for one full hour it has maintained a dignified arch."
>
> —Kenji Miyazawa, "Report," *Spring & Asura*

These are the days I signed up for, though I can't seem to find that book,
that ledger anywhere. All summer I thought I was tending a cottonwood,
then another neighbor breezed by, spoke of my beautiful basswood,
and I nodded as if I had always known the tree's true name. I've been
playing quite a lot of music with no words. That's usually the wrong
choice for me but since summer ended it has been the right choice.
These days are fall days, despite my heroic efforts to keep summer here.
Hummingbirds I mistake for dragonflies, darning needles—I see
now they are hummingbirds, am relieved I planted enough flowers
that held their blooms so late, so they can eat until they are full.
They fly to my neighbors' yard, but that's okay. I love my neighbors.

The Saint of Everything

Saint of the Murderers and Their Dead.
Saint of the Knife-Makers, the Writers,
Saint of the List-Makers and the Self-Congratulatory
Peace-Makers. Too busy. Too tired.
Keeps forgetting: not immortal.
Keeps forgetting: all hierarchies,
All value systems. Saint of Camus
and Saint of the Tree, Saint
of Wetlands, Marshes,
The Oasis Turned to Desert.
Saint of the Innocent
and the Wicked Who Meant
Their Wickedness. Saint
of the Snowstorm
and the Car Spinning
on Black Ice. Saint
of All Singers, Saint
of All Drummers, Saint
of the Humble, Invisible
Painters, Saint for Thieves
and Saint for the Roadside
Shrines, Saint of the Rubble,
Saint to the Crows Shot Out of the Crowns
of Trees. Saint for Travelers
and Those Who Abide,
Saint of Imprisoned Animals,
of Honey and the Bees.
The Saint of Everything:

Fearless, reckless,
stunned, sturdy. Saint
of Mapmakers and All
the Lost. The Saint of Everything
never has time on her hands,
does his work inside
the rules of time.
Busy, exhausted. Happy, lonely.
Open-minded. Heart out of control.
At peace with dying for too many reasons.

There's Nothing Wrong

Once you tell the big lie
All the small lies
Just seem feverish
A trick of art
A trick of the eye
Of the heart
Once you tell the big lie
You can pretend
The small lies
Are just for protection
There's the red horse
Only you see
Babies come back
To life
And roses bloom
Everywhere in the depths
Of your privileged winter
Blues

One of the Old Songs

The guy walked past singing *white bird in a golden cage*
on a winter's day in the rain. One of the old songs,
by the group It's a Beautiful Day. Whatever songs
the radio assigns me, whatever songs strangers sing
as they pass me, those are my songs for the day.
This is my creed, my gospel, my way of trying to stay
in the world I was born into. I sang the song
doing the dishes that night, and it felt right singing
white bird in a golden cage, on a winter's day
in the rain. It was winter, I was white, as I always
would be, I understood myself to be in a golden cage,
large enough to live a whole life in. I understood
it was a beautiful day, and I lived the song in my body
and mind that whole beautiful day.

End Notes

The title "The Heartland, Where the Secrets Are" is a line from Lee Child's *One Shot.*

"Three Things I Asked My Friend" is for Jim Moore.

"The Shield" is for Brendan Keenan.

"A Better Promise" is for Joe Seidel

"The Saint of Abandoned Nurseries" is for Susan Fuller.

"These Days" was written in honor of Nancy Walden and Bernie Kremenak.

"The Butterflies" is for Daniel and Kathleen Bowman.

"Blue Fish Nights" is for Larry, Peggy, Cassidy, Gabe, Sam, Brendan, Molly, Joe, Cordelia, Stephen.

"Not Too Far From Home" is for Jean Adams.

Guardians for this book: Kelly Mowrer, Sam Dillon, Jim Moore, Patricia Francisco, and Mary Francois Rockcastle.